SCAMMER

Dom Hale

Published 2020 by the87press
The 87 Press LTD
87 Stonecot Hill
Sutton
Surrey
SM3 9HJ
www.the87press.co.uk

Scammer © Dom Hale 2020

The moral right of Dom Hale has been asserted in accordance with the Copyright, Designs and Patents Act 1988

ISBN: 978-1-8380698-2-7

Collages by Jessica Widner
Design: Stanislava Stoilova [www.sdesign.graphics]

If we knew the formula we could make our own

Kevin Davies

Sometimes our refusal is in our staying put.

Anne Boyer

CONTENTS

1 Entry Level   7

2 Dust Mite   11

3 Theme Songs   25
  - Delete All   27
  - Domain Name   29
  - Dreams Bonus   30
  - Green Hype Orison   31
  - Hit Counter   32
  - Conveyer Deep   33
  - Click Farm   34
  - Safeguard   35
  - Cloud Pavilion   36

4 Immaculate Blip   39

5 The Noughties   69

1
ENTRY LEVEL

Feeds on a platform, horizon

Only timeline

Branchless

Banking in my windpipe.

Uppity irritant

Shrinkage, fleeting

Down I go.

A veering light

Skyline warded,

Flaky flaky tip off the scuppered

Charging you

Yet again a little hemmed.

2

DUST MITE

In the fridge-freezer of the trillionth sky, our data
        plan screeches
    to a fault and I
               accumulate ice.

I pay-per-click.

That's nice.

Connectivity flows.

This mix is for the lodes and streams.

It's a soft fork. It's that I lay
        down my dowsing rod
    for subtexts and setbacks, and gloze. Nerfing
              the scam
vacuum

at record lows. At record lows.

Loom. Web scrape. Hazing me. Modality
        sidesteps and does not
    refresh my screen on timeout, valued
              corporate accomplice.

And truly knows.

And bluely flows.

And dollar light.

Dollar light and which terrestrial underwater.
      Angels lurk in Litecoin light.
           This catatonic strophe.
                  And continental transfer.
And go on, grant immunity.
      This catastrophic reed.
          Dollars lite and
                sewn at bursting
evil speed.

And now I'm stepping through the street.

And leave all your belongings.

Miracle pinnacle.

Peak everything peak nothing.

I show you the backdoor
          to this sweet
  and new encryption.

Price flux, no words,
          lark lux
      feeling a little
  under the weather, I promise to you now
         I won't give up
      my day job as we brainstorm
on the superdeluxe escalator, getting
  progressively
      terse.

Lovely Frank I escalate.

Is, is.

Wipe away the hyperloop, lurch
   out of this.

Incredible.

Go slow.
         Why type through late
   late carbon
hype. Why
                 skywrite.

Anonymous for days
               and then
   affirmed
under surveillance, valence,
        pinging me
   a hoax. I drop my phone here,
spit at an adjacent adult gamer, collapse
               the viral
       aisle. Unspecified
for nanoseconds,
      peer. In situ singing
   facial recognition, when
           in affinity
                I hack.

And smile. And breathe.

Another mail merge beyond the pile.
              Go clear.

Row back.

Coming soon to a cinema
   coterminous with you,
 I track all the packages, teethe throughout
my small cascade of info, debugging zone
 on zone, clip on clip, skillsets
   to innovatively hone
     alone. Tick-tock, tick. Deep
    web figure of our probability.
      This lyric kills fascists.
 Clicking through a cryptosystem.
   And therefore, fuck,
 imperial night proceeds
from these procedures, arraigning the latest habit of
 extinction, while the final lab technician
lip-reads something crucial
     which concerns the
    causal chain letter.
 The evil skies are CERN's.
      A power of turns and lulls
   returns.

And feeling blinkered
   in the acid rain
     I burn.
 No words.
Do better.
  PR weather
 portal
   birds on
      birds. The plain
   debris lets you too
     prophesy, and I
   watch Season Two
 of *Firefly*.

And getting mortal.

And hatemail floods in melodies the inbox.

What year is this?

>	Big Bird clocks and mock-ups.
Handfuls.
>	Nulls.

And refuse for the hypersubject.

Serco crowdsale
>	in a zany
>	daydreamlet or four.

And hours seat themselves on aspects of the sea:
Ursa Minor, kids,
   is long since undetained.
>			Thank fuck.
>		Don't @ me.
>	Jet set PVA latte kaput.
>			Not sorry.

Phoning it in, that we were flurrying
too many away from the matter
>		out of hand, or nearly, showing
>		our working:

you speak to me of negligible glitches, missing numbers:

you check my bandwidth for me, lumen human:

you escape rope out of Victory Road

bye tempest
Boom in.

File under
the cutbacks,
done.

To insure the zoom back in
and more. :)

I miss your voice. Look where it's gone to.

Speedread.

We feel for us.

We loophole users
use the force.

And shyly
I transact.

And now I'm syncing in the street.

All daily scales, all fearful hands are in
               the viewfinder.
You better have burn heal.
      No words. Floating
  your ideals to floating voters,
      tripping off the temporal balcony
  in Nikes.
            Sorry
            not sorry, POTUS.

This mix is for your habits and dreams.

This solves the scalability bug.

I note the interplanetary elision.

A blessing in the skies disguised.
We're here
        for it
                lol hi.
Decelerate for good.
        And you do you. And
  enter tab left
the citizens' first trillionaire,
        showing your working out
  a little file flits over SoundCloud.

Pinnacle miracle.

Peak nothing
ha, peak all.

Scan, scan
  for a change.
                Flow brittle,
        microbead.
Carbon-sucking over the meltwater
  Freon
        spree
arriving, amazing
                blip IRL
Unmanned a standard issue panic
  Skim, skim
                Track changes

I guess I just
   wasn't made
         for these mites.
             It lands.
We stew in that misprision, Google
   vision.

And allocate me nodes and moods.

And just like that I'm over it.

West melancholy
             heaps up
   over east melancholy
over left melancholy
         into EuroMillions.
             Emit it.
Bodyboarding, peeps. Skim-read.
   The kyriarchs will single out
a certain quark.
             To seed,
to torque.
Flooring it, thorough
         the architectonics of a turquoise
   heaven: in San Diego
             wherever
         does the day go.
Shadowban
the ache from every solar plexus,
         finesse the tessellated weeks
   or cover
them in Play-Doh.

A puncture in the membrane.

So I descended moodily
to Silicon Valley, thinkpieces
        falling softly
                like sociable
  hallucinations,
installations.
                Well-won winds,
        when will you glow.

No words.
  I love you and the life that is

A further shape that should be free.

Game over.

Standby
even
song.

Don't @ me,
think tank.

Hedge alphabets.

Mayday even out the song.

Decelerate for good.

Flotsam bot, a flock of not.

I
wondered
only

as a clod.

A flock of not. A launching spot.

3

THEME SONGS

• Delete All

Here I am the doormat of my track,
fucking Bezos
chatbots, frenemies
in Bowser's closing castle.

Telic, telic.

Command override.
And the surreptitious violent
anthem
fade command override.

Cursed liberal images
glide across a stately screen. Password-protected
renounce gurgle
demand the supply.

You're my best friend
in a world we
must upend.
In worlds.

Life-ish
cauterised, send me current location, send
the elegance
of sober
teeth lit incalculable drone kaleidoscope.
Beautiful novae
blurting Serco,

send me current
currency rate
ultra nostalgia right up to the secateurs.

Legible
pieces of the grid system, convoluted into sunny.
Share location as per
demand the supply
lines and songlines and lawns
never held so mutually
a damage counter.

And hit space pink + white undo.

And prepare me carefree
welfare, speeder
bike slowing
down fair-weather
ends.

What a wonderful kind of day.

Children of the future
age, experience the starry pole. Feed forward
lovely boy.
Feed back to the group.

• Domain Name

Collateral lunchtime is achieved.
Everybody else is searching for everybody,
reaching a settlement and scudding
frictionless over the septic threshold.
Help me to help you. Slogans
of planet light. I was fucking
with these young professionals. I was
fucking with these young professionals when we swept
together in the feted atrium like.
I'll be there for you.

And since the paintjobs borrow crises,
blood and sand. Force quit copy,
blood and sand. Force quit

then I sit up
on my tuffet and sing
these. No two at first in-house for curds
and whey, the rhythm of the street. Intel outside.
Heatwave, trail heatwave.
Shrink-wrap survey.

• Dreams Bonus

Gazed laughably negations and a slump.
The tuning down and turning off.

Because the, view the Burj Khalifa.
Rehistoric altitude,
an outlook.

A downturn in my throatful, typecast
ease once the airport terminal furnishes
preoccupations with a bit
and peace. All-out protein.

I'm curved over an icon in the park, plural
soon and order-breaking, typing what will
talk itself into this.
Procedures of the free, a heap of monikers.
Procedures of the ambient and me.

Primary brain cell
Blackpool Tower N334AA.

So we got everyone together.
Hypnosis for the civil aisles, a conceptual
breeze and common courtesy. I would hold you like it,
helping you to help you telecoms scramble.
A sentence not yet pesticides.

Halo of Finnieston.

• Green Hype Orison

Upkeep for daydreams.

In hiding
representatives know what
I'm not.

Sinking
the hypocrites of iMessage.

I am part route.

And what too were the pasts,
taken together. Luck a lotus corridor.
An earful. And what too were the motile.

That the socialisers may yet be secured.

Lately fortuitous.
Lately fortuitous
sky clarion big data.

• Hit Counter

There go the systems analysts, the demigods
on Wall Street, the profiles
that you meet. Prepare there additionally the big hitters
(you borrow my hand),
the limpid scarecrows and straw public of the lyric
eye. Carcinogens in song,
skip track. And get
along with each other, vegetable memory like
as a century didn't permit to breathe.

Reboot me, plenty identifications. O pedestrian.

Malpractice
on a crushing scale. Stir it.
A hot take
over accountability, fuck me.

The couriers collate themselves.

Regreen softly because.
Windfall.

- Conveyer Deep

So rip the payoff.

Contactless
macroclimate
I feel it glow
the Pleiades,
the self-advanced.
Show us
your fangs.

Go live

the more
the more

you suck.

Magic trash is voided.
Herbaceous borders
and a grieving sign
we are the rigmarole
my net worth
worthy of the meltwater.

A super soaker and a cloaking device.

• Click Farm

Into the authorisation.

So typed your thinking thought.

Percentile
file a gloopy populace, a carton
of cartoons.
Veering away from my antagonist
a stupid amateur.

We fell in love on Skype
a couple of years after the crash.

Sup. Sup,
you will be hearing from my antagonist.
Oil it all.

That way lies the event horizon, land
of the fee.

Headwinds oncoming, oncoming gameplay
soon to a cinema.
No words.

Clouds point   over the vaxxed
          globe with the storm
themes luridly of clouds.

• Safeguard

Beautiful amateur uses cookies.
I'm published by the acid rain.

It isn't the last you've seen
of the future
thinking this is bitesize
guzzling my buzz food
revising the greenhouse effect.

Two-bit fractal moi.

I never knew that, post-crash
I channel hop
I flop.

• Cloud Pavilion

    Select recipients
    know your bandwidth
    choose your starter!

    I hydrate.

    Solvent lyrics and an asthma attack.

    Help us to help us, drawing lots
    oneiric in the oil drum.

    Earthing linguistics.
    The knowledge of all fonts.

4

IMMACULATE BLIP

Completed me.

Empaths,
click through.

Circulating online
it snowed clients.

We were legible as avenues
apportionments

an earworm
IP

s/o users
helping users
We demolished my brain

influx on
influx

polycosmic earworms

skipping through the planetariat
cumulus addict
bright with progress
off le nebuliser

wat %
doss, multistorey

breath may
undo
rising sea
levels
no confidence
this mite this
single-use
plastic

I miss your voice. Look where it's gone to.

Is, was.

Telecrats storm
the latter
embassy

flitting
under geopower

Bad algorithm

prospects :)

ecocidal
ideation.

and smile.
and breathe.
no words.

fascists fucking everywhere

eating a cornetto
w/ you
along some whippy
promenade in the
societies
Ctrl

knock-knock
AdBlock

Too true
to be good.
Print screen.

Think monkeypox
feeling in the incubator
derp.

Is counselled.

Laters.

Too bad
to be true.

My defunct Mii.
View media
my clavicle
my sappy avatar

Lucrative Esc
The sympathetic system
vailing profits
and i say pay

How to feint
before emergency powers

Fake it now

O doorway, hacktivist

Newsflash
collateral patio…

Memo fusses
hissy fit
i've got receipts

beyonsense!
beyond
theory i
Upgrade to Premium

weary movie
floss.txt
Inside
blips on the
re
cycle
mock

w/e
favouriting a wrong thing
on standby
never
hyperlooping, troops.

Long
livestream.

This is astonishing
consciousnesses :)
interning

interning

to overlap
which hurt
to overhaul

Timeless enzyme

Inlet, outlet
we're beautiful
we're workers

how shitty, ducking
easy punchlines

could this
payment be a scam?

humhumhum

inter
paddocks
visit Clare

go pick
candy
Crush

bit bot
blippy
nits, the

house of commons after
arson

Shell
crowing at your Meatless Monday

lurking
trolls and vices, heretically

LAN

⚥ ☞✞☂☺✋☠♪ ♦☀✋♦♦   ☒🏳✞

attempered

to teh sorrows of

rare-earth

the fucking
smurfs

sometimes I scar
myself, and

wit on earth
lmao

Clever. Ambient panorama.

In the muddle of
this half-life.

Anything is process.

hope to cope

and cope
with hope.

Coolly optimising

Micromanage
flux blurt doxa
this latest
.doc
of the
attention
economy

your old friend's
Rented sky

Echelon of pain. A pain
in the stubs of your toes

Easier over the megacity.

Flit, structure of a person
Pronto

go platinum
growth

little
social networks

w/e
hyperdebt
to let, it's
super

effective
Gone and it is a moment.
Summer energy a day.

There is this ruse in a centre.

sorry this is long.

Ochre layby;'#
retooling
:(lulling the verticals

The mix exits
into particles.

I feel an energetic rainbow towards the equinox.

Foreach loop.

No words
on words.

No words.

The comments section of the song.

Cloudburst moxie.

eyes wrack the arch
see hierarchies
liquefy

melt
a dear mannequin
snoozing, supervisor of immiseration

the lyric assay

every fascist out the fucking cubicle

i must loaf forever

The avenue
is topical

Googlable

Top Score, these
gorgeous notes

Je suis
resource
war, on tour
Caroline clownishly ascends

yr fyred.

Weeklong appliance, turned up
on the work surface

ty
flatline, flatline.

Is, will.

Leave
behind the

nanosettings

Prism
flocks don't
lull me. x

McFlurry of angels

Wave of nausea
by the photocopier.

Faking
a living, tops,

in that department
cycling
celestial

updates, horrible
memetic
spells

and bored af

With all the time in the world.

boys, alas!
Pan naps.
alas, yob.

Come with, thanks in advance.

come w/
unemployed
domain
name unlearning love

☹🕬✋☼🎗✌🎗🎵 ❄🏳 ☹🏳✞🕬

the end of
lyf

but
no. The property of Cuadrilla

A pun shaves
off th windscreen

A government worker
or a curb of light

Within limits.

homing
crises
unplant lop, go
meh.

You are astonishing
like language, like

out of
language

not from
concentrate

summery
given

I say to Chelsea Manning

What does not change / is the will to climate change

hmm…
2infinity +blond

That's rich.

A gated

Centuries chlorinate.

Hoodwink. How few or how

many windows the city

No messing.

so
it
is here

to tell
you

you
are loved

This slaps.

teetering
stat, Antiwork Thursday.

And keep it down in there.

Timor mortis conturbat me

Added to the dataset
CEO on a spit

this signs
that i
am here
@

libidinal yep
cut the, flush the
Barclays ogres
Raking

care
on any day
u want
to die
see
this
as
ily

like there's no tomorrow

cut it out. Sit tight

We get out of the car.

regale me
on your lunchbreak
i'll regale you as soon as we get in.

To be oil+

be safe
in the overflow

lowkey
br0ken, touching my face
negative
incapability

heart murmur
inland empire
soft power

Live up

next time
round
These lives
detained

As nexus now
u typed

Sign out.

to be held
you

Wishy-washy cash
     lyrics, lyrics
   lyrics lush.
  Spell celerity.

Try again.

Sustainable workload.

in the kill chain
in the short
run.

to be
held
IRL

inside
the currency
the end reset

5

THE NOUGHTIES

Don't spray it, scrolling downward to the final
        boss,
                          bilaterally
the degrees skyrocket.
    Clock it.

Here I go in alphabetical order
                      apropos of nothing
    metabolising golden spikes
laboratories of aether
capable and positively dazzling with questions
        pleased to meet you, earthling
                either/or.
Hearting this at
once. Continuance. Like half-life.

There were these emissions.

                      Traceable, I
    type in real time, hitting a nerve
                from end to end to end
What's happening?
    Error and trial
        Clipping the forecast
    autonomous flows
publicise a sweet external logic
    deletions from the aircon
    How to snort my love songs
                Nope, nope
neon eon
    ricochets galore, switch user

still on Facebook
      scarify
      an apology for.
We'll see.
  Theoretically speaking
sustainable day
      Snorlax used Snore!
  Sustainable day
training my dragon in the tidal heating.
       I know, Io. We
       eat as we go.

You're my send-up. We've got loads of time.

Unreserved seating
    in the holding pattern
the next few years are probably the most important
    in our something
in my infinite provisional happy place
  and you tweet
there is a moonbow *flaring somewhere*

            Lip sync, playmate, thinking
            what I'm thinking, mind map follows
                 mind map
        make a mental note
                      my Poké Flute,
moot point.
        Get Jr to a facility
is voided.
        Fake muse.
                     This placeholder kills fascists.
                I won the internet
         and adulting
        We inform to regret you
Another thinkpiece about pending
persevering with the throwback
                        seamless
boomerang.
                Numb and number
            come the intern obscurantists
                    all along the mantelpiece
        ringfenced fantasia
Econarcissisms certified inert
and so a long jump backwards

            Enormous blisses where the fun starts
                    vanished
         Feeling 4% and sheepish
             either
                     frack your bacne,
Daphne of the Evian
    or fraudulently

determine at which precise point the junior minister
        became radicalised
                      Harping
    on inside the Global North
        Polling stations
                altered, ready
        salted. The info dump
enclosed in smallprint.
I ghost, you ghost. You

thickly have five minutes. You have a century.
    You have twelve years.

It is the Square of Four Sads
where a vigilant icon declares
        fucking disaster porn for ever after.
    I'm serious.
        And after an incontrovertibly downcast
    rummage through time
        methodologies congeal by the toaster
        the satellites convert post-internet
help pick out
        a Minneapolis sidewalk in Street View
    for good measure
Is it time for reprogramming
squawk a sentinel species
            in the logjam of the other world
Normative sporks.
    Deniers roll up electably and we concentrate
    all our scrupulousness
        on the shoot of an arcsecond.

Evening Maggie.
Evening Simpkin.

                    The mistake is to panic
though there's truth in the rush and the objects.
Offline is mine. The sage
in its wage fronting the almshouse
                There's pleasure here. The judder.
    Abandoning the MET Office, you
consolidate all your debts into one
        low-cost repayment
forget about the memo, irony's moonbow
                    reverses financialised
and here you are
      battening at last on deep responsibility
            taking these interim steps, careful
          to dodge the guilty tripwire,
                  towards the Outer Rim.
Miracle ballots.

Still, what's the forecast WALL-E
    out of the friendly woods like fleeting tweezers
   out of the stuffed crust
wave goodbye to the technocrat
               abandoned veteran
we're history one minute
then we're not.

                              Every clause
    cut duckling
                    obviously not a calamity song
the day before tomorrow
        because the teleprompter's always been
        professionalised
and you owe a lot of emails to a lot of people
    Every clause
    a tab against despair.

Eleven yesses, seer, eleven
years

Seems legit.

    Pathfinders cross from one end of
        the ISBN to the blueprint, hacks smoking
   behind the call centre vermillion swimming
    in and out of sync
            at times
A journalistic twitch through buggy
        diagnostics
   Self-charging hybrid
            and Mystic Meg
lisping in the participatory installation.
   Another hooked apology for piety.
       Scan, scan. Blocked
Keep it clean
Forget the spiralizer
   I said I wouldn't talk about it
and I'm not going to, buster

                      That would be far too
                far too easy
    Stop-start
None the wiser send me
    on my way.

        You never want to leave
        yourself nor will you. Max potion
Astride a single search engine
                you can't pimp the loss.
    Very annoying.
You recommend me to the climate primate
        Flippant clipart. Blocked
From a yurt by Lake Geneva
                  I grew my fingernails
        and accustomed
    Recalling conveyances, the love required
to run the browser when the clocks never
        go back, always approaching.
A streaming excess accommodates the rest.
Wait for it.

Sorry for the delayed response
sorry to disappoint, you pass me your first
                backward glance
        at the lifeworld
            at the U.N. singsong
                    multifeedbacks
feel free
        alarming the alarmists
        hands-on
off the hook
    cupping a policymaker in aquamarine
                tragic pixelated
edgelord out of the airlock

    Like half-life
I sink into a peapod with the relevant
                risk thresholds
        static telematics, fossils
sorry for cross-posting
    stupidly nostalgic for the fucking noughties.

Huge if false. The most embarrassing
    bit of junk mail I have ever seen. Jobs
                and growth, some pointers.
        The grand scam. From
    disinformation, free speech
                frees Peach. In opposite

land. A rant and a chant. We believe
it's possible
to have effective, natural and safe
cleaning products that
don't cost the earth.
Alexa, it's 2017
and yesterday's all gravy
Flippant clipart
corroding in that hammock
The aisle
useful
Of poises
Meg and Mog and Reese's Pieces
Asking for a friend
I am a ballpark figure
The sputum of Westcheap gives way
fatally to a
coracle of rules
Godspeed
You speedread
Making
out with Ingram
Frizer

Oh my goodness gracious,
what you can buy off the internet
in terms of overhead photography!

In terms of the gyrotheodolite.

In terms of a zit of the equinox.

Keep a place for me.

Like there's no tomorrow.

On your shoulders,
    on your shoulders nudging towards
the end of the implementation period
       and manmade
for good measure, miracle ballots
            Xenophanes regards a
  teletsunami of burger sauce
O carbon handprint
    we're not meant to leave the world
we're meant to save it
            geeking out over the pivot
by the precipice
               we'll see.

Algae rhythm.

A sky's a clause.

Asking for a friend.

                                That's enough.
We're meat again, don't know where
            Wat Tyler, stat harvester
    what the fascist managers
    did to my little brother
Solid aridity.

Yeah in tandem I could

wish I might

upload a sweeter playlist too.

                        The comeback.
Bit of a slender distraction, puckish and
        peckish
     hanging on
  to the reboot, mouth-to-mouth

Personages fleeing the Peace Corps in the 2020s

Superhabitable spreads

It may be cancelled
        Broca's area evacuated
                but my friends haven't given up
A counterfactual expanse inside the threnody of Piglet

Nanotech authentically
souped-up in the infinity pool says time was a
myth.

You're kidding.
                        A splash of calm
                        A splash of calm

    And catch my drift.
I just want to be able to do something
but I'm up to my neckerchief.

    Stay woozy,
cell phone. The Twin Towers
        leech quite beautiful today. Burnout
                Baking by your top solar array
            I caricature the jeremiad
    Get spammed
             A loving hand
        This is an incomplete self-own

    And yet a dash
divorced from their reality
        The ensuing kudos

      A corridor of power.
  Let's face it
Siri, tinyurl.co
      m/y44kdbf6 sanitised. And you are
        properly the fishhook
  Gulf. Lean into it.
    Take everything
        impersonally. Cute.
    Seems legit.
  This shit demands redaction.
More fool me.
      A katabatic wind.

      You have nothing to lose, the earth has everything to gain.

      For the foreseeable.

      Volvic cleromancer and the sovereign foodie.

      In the pipeline.

      You do it all now, but at a glacial pace.

      And not shrink-wrapped

above the pole.

And not for content products.
    Prep one of us for reconstruction

  Ballooning yet endangered, stranger.
The gig economy or something
    Joyous rhyming book exploring opposites

        Microwave me. Pop me in the
     microwave. Be worldly-wise,
       BP... urlz
            s.com/ZMdTg

By a thread
you scribble back to say
    If there is always memory in working-class life
    it is because things are always being taken away
Warping the pitfall in which I got my education

        Now you crop up
        Now I.

            So go ahead millennials
                    giving what I'm
hearing in the blogosphere
    a wide berth dope linguinism.
                            Luck. Heck.
Non-refundable
                neo-eon
biome alone.
They scream only of Antarctica.
    Fuck death.
            Alphabetically
anointed loser
hoovering carbon out of the pressured
                            atmosphere, hoovering
up the teleologies
            upswing data. Go team
            eroteme.

    For night
    uninterrupted
love
    parsecs
                white noise, famous
        lost
worlds.
    Chewie, we're home.

At its last click
tagging along, tagging along
        it's cool with me.
Which raises the question from the dead.

And underneath the halogens
kids go free.

        And underneath.

    I can't even.

You see, the claim that we are now post-truth is in fact
pre-truth. You see, I'm aftermath
    all the way down. Working 9
        to 9. Dead Sea normalcy.
            Core *InfoWars*. Four laws.
    Thank you for coming to my TED Talk.

What is this 'dick chainy'
        and where can I get one?

The cinematic event of the old millennium.

    It's like the Illuminations in here.

Steve's job.

    My inhaler shatters in my hands.

        Unbelievable
            Style it out.
Lying in the network
        will you please stop
    sealioning me
Scamper, scamper
        Rigs on stilts.

                    Article 370
ADHD wittily
                              spreading out
          along the briny beach.
                         I resent that.
               All at once
                    the debate
wades into me, Siri
                         I re-sent that
          Give or take
                    Cease and desist
                         A kind of cough
disarms the global cop
          Artisanal
                         oil platform,
                    higher up.

Just a reminder that
     the good life of a
     wit isn't a warfare in Epcot
               Retconning my deeper memorabilia
Retconning the noughties
     the noughties uncapitalised
     when this must be the take, they say
          You've got to laugh
          into the foreign policy of the axolotl. Cute.
Through a mouthful of aubergine emoji

I am the cryptic keyboard warrior du jour
                who sees, unsees all sides like
      Come to your censors
               abscond, absconding
post-dizziness from Sensorvault
                  I will fucking bite you
avows the first ever black hole image
      Ket muttering
on the rewild show
in the Google data center
        Time to specialise
      They have the plants
      but we have the power.

              Het up. It bugs me, overhead live
wire, as I trip over your coattails
          into the way
the world works. Don't chicken
out, Cummings suffocating swift.
Jack carries a pail of water
          with me in it. A pterodactyl
      passes over Sellafield. That's messed up,
and presently from just outside the vestry
           we overhear the data
weaponisers chuckling intensely
      A real money-spinner
      Flayed persuadables kiss you through the
          hole of this vile wall.
The truth is telling me at this point.

Our tablets were sufficiently committed so as to be,
unless we found ourselves in the throes and deluges
of certain unsynthetic moods, almost entirely
bereft of pleasure, joy,
        nothing of the life we need,
            but we got them over the line, so to speak
        and at last could stew in our aureate rectitude

For the foreseeable.
You feel the knowing. Samesies.
Mindfuck.
    I really don't endorse this candidate
                Vista
    One of us is freaking possessed.
            The assent.
    Make it up as I go along
in a crevice of the party, mea tulpa,
kicking off with Edward Snowden
              Welcome to fandom.
    Renege on the vague
More power to you
        trying to please everybody, fibre
            and fibre pleasing
    no one. In the marketplace of ideas
              chucking it down
my molecules of freedom,
    let's stay here for a spell.
    Go
                blow a gasket.
            Tweet the rich
Chernobylite lite and the height

    of good manners
        A zero-hour
when disaster capitalists and sociopaths
waltz right in then scam you once again
  Defenestrate yourself
    avec the most desultory of curlicues
      when
        I'm bone idle.
    Full of lulls

  In sum:
 So what actually *is* my emotional age?
Scan, skim
  Foam in the logos
    With a petty piece of katabasis
With a grim carload of crocuses
       I do declare
    my sudden enemies
 are made of straw
   Gulp. Doggy paddle.
   Open mind. You've got
     to laugh. Soothe @:

Leap anecdotally into the next clone sleep.
   And catch my drift.
  And underneath.
Please don't tell anyone how I live.
     Pics or it happened
   Box-fresh perspectives
adjusted for inflation
  maintain the stalemate

                    Tweety in the mine
               Diode, diode
For good measure
      you're it.

               It's July and
               I'm in love
sitting by the observatory
        itineraries of clouds
               itineraries of catalysts.
Heart this.
                    As lief.

        The underlying.
               From time to time
        sentimental middlemen and Dora the Explorer
horse around on Reddit. You're it.
A mushroom from the Minister for Loneliness
                    tones my commissioner down
               indicates the programmatic
                    and khôratic future
        would have passed anyway.
Therefore I am still
                    lactose ebullient
        Milkshakes in their faces
        Chameleon liquefaction of the
Tex-Mex non-exit

> Zits of time
>
>   mfw
> sky smells
>
>   of disinfectant
> issueless predicaments
>   cloudy with a chance
> hieroglyphics lifting from the screen
>   normalities of
>   money drizzle
> down my plucky throat

And so on. And catch their drift. All
        hinging on your gastric band. And
                out the other. All
        breaking ranks for Swaziland.
Nootropic Elixir
        to boost my brain performance
Designed by Silicon Valley-based neuro
        and bio-hackers

                        Napalm Eton.
        No words.

                                Scummed over.
                Ordinary hardworking environments
        Petering out
                A powerless nonanonymous
        citizen who broke no laws,
                who broke some laws.

    Pied piper of the Kremlin.
Don't patronise me, pilot. Patronise
me, matron. I reckon
        this might just be my personal best
                tantrum of the spheres.
    And give me good riddance
        of my present grievances, showing you
no wisdom in my movement.
    A windfarm I find warm. Quack.
        They have a situation here.
                Peter Thiel picks oakum. To be
        discontinued. Ahead of time
        I favourite all your errors
                in the mirror, I'll
        stay here for a spell.
Headfuck. A rich hiccough of
    clickbait, Houyhnhnm refuse
gets sponsored by the
                Edinburgh Futures Institute
        Expungéd sponges.
    What really gave me gyp
was the low-budget trailer for the biopic
        of Northern Rock
Haranguing every single one of your odd
    socks in a dream link
                Duck-billed platitudes

Lockdown. It's possible to click on this
but not the half of it.

    Don't be evil. Scunnered. OK, be
    fractionally evil

                Go and lose work.
          This is the mouth of a poet's grind.
          To crudely paraphrase, I assume
with great sobriety the role of gate guardian
outside Cape Canaveral. Scambaiting solo.
      A checkpoint mutilates my heart. Shoot
          Patronise me, patron,
                    stick it in Helvetica, fee-skimming
by another staff toilet in another martyred Starbucks
          Really getting down to it, soupçon
                to soupçon
      3D printing fourteen freedoms in your heatstroke
                you resolve gracefully
        to respect other passengers
            who drive you round the bend, the
    instant wave of instant messages
Cambridge Analytica harvest
            something gently from my breeches.
    I'm only really alive when I'm
        pressed inside the poem, blister
            Kony 1312

As the arbiter of carbs I'm pleased
        to have met you. Nope
              Harm eaten. Cross-ref it,
          zoning in through air-built thoroughfares
        the elector ate the electorate

      I feel you, meliorist,
pinging outside Holyrood
   accredited in Clitheroe, my hired
behaviour had a sort of leavening effect
     on the car park
       think glacial POV
   thinking happily of hitching

       Time after
time I mistook the mysterious ticking
    noise for you
  repeatedly
  stubbing your toe on the wormhole
  Glaucoma for the loner.
       A workless household.
    Survival of the shittest.
From a technicolor outcrop I do
  resonate with you and you
    and even you, flush before the mural
  of your next demurral. Inaccurate blip,
it got to me. Relatable. Standing
   with the Stansted 15,
  partner, then wilfully proceed to bottle
      somebody's career poems
   in a fragrant reverie
    I've tabled it.

                    Airtime.
                Enjoying airtime.
Leaked documents hit back before
    you pensively freecycle them
            It fits. Ye have frozen the preening
    of skiing (humorous). Dragged
through a hedge forwards
                Laminar flow
    throughout the BioQuarter, dissent messages
flounder at my most impressionable.
    Track changes, mangers
                Bunker EU.
    I solemnly swear
    that I am up to bunk off,
hunker down, insulated
            from the block periphery.
                Not not a soundbite, right.
    Time's up against the intranet.
But then you would say that.

From Central Pier, like Rodefer my late processor, I DM
the pneuma of further bars to make lavish my encystment
            Whoosh. I am a struct.
    You make a noise complaint
                wishing you could bilocate
    Retrace some steps
in the ragged purlieus of the
              media blackout. Targeted ad
        The oldest attention seeker
                in a century. Extort

the shit out of your chosen CEO, point being
    Little and often. Little and often.
      What the dickens
           these logistics
Athirst in the great Amerikan desert, I guess I'll bail.
        Too small to fail. Time was money so
           go timeless for a sec, lap it up
    against the here wherein the real fightback starts
    Hand me the Tupperware of chlorinated tofu
           A bailout for a basic
glitch, qubit, when moral panic swashes
    listenably. Then HR give me herds of grief
      Emit time, pupper, walking
           in the park: let brass neck
      follow brass neck,
    air mile bail out air mile, or go off
           Imitate the imitator.
           I stared into a dim hole.

    And the good news is that you don't need
  to be extremely punctual
           for neighbourhood gatherings.
I might slide in there by 7pm, with my potluck dish
      (spinach salad) and it will be
  all just fine. Knowingly rerouting
  autotune, my moonlighter, and leased
    to meet you. My absentee. Phones
  contemplate the aether, aether
contemplates the drones. What-ho Pelosi,
in additive rain always impending

            to be seeming. Your car
                 has been dispatched.
                         Aesthetic innocence.
And over sidles another punctuation mark
    in the shape of an event,
    a sappy buyout left to
                scan, bite me with the Gamma Knife
       hit me with the Paris Agreement
     wing me with the trending tweets
                    Driven from distraction.

It's midwinter and we snuck over the hedge to
        Little Sparta in our boxers once again
Realising in the fifth and
    final act we'll break this pact
meme jackal, young professional
                    jack-in-the-box
a thinking cap for your
                favourite asshat
Oh flip.

       I am
       who I remind you of,
       old friend. And near

                      Downwardly mobile.

We're at the cliff edge of evasion or accountability
    when, with staggering composure, you
        force my shoe on with the shoehorn.
                Cop out. Upend the deep end,
            dream your follows, debtor
    Nix boosts over there.
A quick-fix sexes up a blooper for their politesse
    A blastocyst slopes off into the gaining mist
        Peak intercropping.
        Peak disincentivised.

    The shuffle function.
I am the doyen of the tinfoil flag
    and as such deserve a solid incubating.
        Boom. O twister of handouts.
Embourgeoisement from the potholes of a
    lower echelon was unarguably heaven sent.
    Psych. A drawbridge, pulling up in Wonderland.
Dealing with these instincts and the lie of the
    right timeline. A golden urge. A newsclip
        in reverse. Sunburst. Sike. Shot
    up a couple of family values. Weapons-grade
    communications muted as I notate
in the latest available data
    An astronomical phenomenon.
    Time finishes the uncomfortable song
        of an idiot but I keep at it forever
and my hireability goes through the roof.

Sit up
>   and tweak the whorl
>   denial. Gulp. Blocked. I appear
>   to have failed to purge
>   my poem of evil. I have yet
>   to decarbonise. Sit up
>   Arbitrary decade in the liberal colostomy
>   Liquidity limping after the catastrophe
>   502 Bad Gateway
>   nginx
> The literal just lost to me
>   Nostalgics
>   for toujours

It goes without saying
>   some of the mistakes were basically palatial
> I disabused my wiser supervisor
>   hyperlinks lighten
>   the coroners brighten
>   what's pasta is pasta.

>   Clerical
> alterity feeling
>   stratospheric on the runway.
> Pally before one of us got subpoenaed

>   And how will you insist?
> An imploding scroll

Liberal gibbets
It had been a happy meal by all accounts, the way
    the monkey puzzle gleamed in the
  light of your paragraphs
How I vaporised, a little south of Auckland
               How you personally
    beacon through
      a livestream to baulk at

where elites and counter-elites arrange
to meet.
              Imploding scroll
      Becks and chalices
multiply on the outskirts of the maize maze
Feeling properly forlorn on last
    looking into Manson's *Adjunct*
at a junction in the gluten age of marginalia.
              Are, are
    terraforming
going without saying
        trapped a nerve.

I get struck off. A poem as short
    as this night-time will be
A tranche in the manicured sky.
    We can do it, we're going together
        No worries.
        And really I must miss my EMA, dearest
Open the prisons. Visceral, scram

This pulp is seductive. I have made it
        an idol of my addiction
     a gloss, but I know that it's cool to let go of it too
Rip the security tag off and bolt. That's class.
               Self-medicate, throw
     out ourselves
          for the best. For the best

Save a space
for me, handsome. I awoke with the
     broke and all in bad
           time, data meets society.
       That old chestnut.
I contribute a contribution to the P2P economy
facilitate all the discussions, plucking
up the courage to tuck into a ripe satsuma
     at the cloud roundtable.
         Anomalous fuss, anomalous.
I clicked there to start my free trial today.
Today I started my free trial by clicking there.
     Faster than fascists and all in time for the
        Chadwick Report, all in
time for 7 billion star jumps on the set menu.
           Lip service, paid.
    Lip service, paid.
        Workplace ready
     I oscillated all Tuesday, that is on the spot.

Hold the fort.
Hold that thought.

                Cologne riot. On autopilot you
     should see this as an opportunity
       Steadfastly unrelatable
Fetching up the sore imperatives
              of a far-flung classroom
            I now hasten to add.
   It's been real. The big reveal.
An evening's not the end of this world or another, sir
      Where will you scamper?
         A dead cert.
  A snap decision.
What time is it, Mr. Wolf?
     A little birdy told you
    it is a bit of a grey area after all, this
           minding your own business
   Hiya, hyena.
Feeling pretty funny
           Guess I'll die.
Wakefulness, futurity, a not uninjured pasture
    Why, aorta?
           Deepfakes in spates present
              themselves for observation
   Don't look at me, I spit out crudo too.

      Well, well
in secret you pronounce yourself
the outreach officer for the
    pick 'n' mix

apocalypse, don't let on.
    Hell yeah. Doss. All the people
   that fall out of a life. Barcode drama.
If this is wrong, I don't want to be right.
The project manager
   manages the project
           Get on
BT-WiFi-with-FON.

  Well, well
    unhinged in the Gulf Stream,
working furiously on my manuscript
         I have paid and displayed.
   How unpresidential of me.
           Lonely neutral,
   torrid in my costume
       Room for a little one?
  Poetry's a thankless task.
   Back it up. Shut it down. I scry twi
tter.co
   m/to
      mcrom
            ptonh/stat
  us/11331
    0269
       546684
  4160
  So much is for you. I love you. *Thank you*.
Thread:

       Placid rain, Urania,

reel off the unabstracted now
    Sunwise into widdershins
      To bed.
               Refer us. Free from.
Keep cropping up for one another.
    Into the click farm, mister
           It positively becomes the auditor.
    What the actual fuck?
A re-mark is poesie. Free from
           My paraffin alias.
        Keep cropping up.

    Keep amniotic.
Targeted ad. Broken like
you should be, yanked
    in this direction
Sowing discord early
I have flown twice, there
and back, since 2012

                        Let that sink in.

Put off morning.

            My bluer iris
        plied against the rick

The time is right, or *isn't right*
    but comic timing keeps.

Just a reminder that
to hack a bunch of Anglophone poetry, nutting
in the woods, you must first

We're all coming up.

And then to an approval rating, which is the most
middling since sliced

O you cowards, O my gatekeepers!
        Flashing before a sovereign body
this dreaming has been removed for further study
    Keying 4x4s
        keying the ectoplasm sector
Premature political capital
        Keying violent stimulants
    and I can't stress this enough
my problematic homework ate my homework
        Huge undo
I enclose everything I've ever written more than you

Sussed out

Thankfully shellacked
abreast yon chatbox
                          break the bank

This is not only a phase.

At 13:55

                an internal vacancy
sways docile in the
legendary winds of Flint.

        Lawn war, scintillating
           no time

like the present

Stuck outside the loss adjusters

                fabless
Fuckers that we hate

        On fire in our optimism.
                Zeroing

A multipack of toxins.
You bathe your stick insect to this

            impulse buy

You take the personality quiz. Same.
I was a worker. You were a worker.
Daddy it's time.

Get on my wavelength. Liveable
Break even, SZA

Flinch. Then insulate your timeshare

Witness Hunt and Javid
walk the burning plank

Globally responsible.

And Bill, this lint we lately scrutinise
    it must surely be true though

Woop. Bump. Going spare
        over a memory stick
            in front of a window of opportunity

    Neutralized in Hatay,
the echoing chamberman

        A feathered jump out of your skin.
        So fake it
          true. That catfish, airtime tinyur
    l.com/y68t
      dd6u

At 15:35

    the administrator of the narrow
garden asserts a pitiable monopoly on so-called
      innovation. Backup

  off the shelf. Whatever's best.

At your behest. And inoperably
from the commuter belt,
   I hope this disappears.

A metabolic gift. The pro-state
prostate. Punching through the firewall
    Adani later
  let me off
      essentially unworthy of regard

    Encounter turbulence.
      Still going. Hard relate,
     pitmatic plankton.

  You lie and you say you do
  with a smile on your face
A rent instalment. The great filter.

      Reject my bio-kin at last
    and jet off to the hills

A landlord, tailing. You leave
  all my belongings there
    and rend
   my mime
Knowing poetry was bigger than the Anthropocene

and all the grant capture opportunities
                        it swung into our lives
                            Accreting quietly in the creative economy

---

It's processing.

                        Meanwhile
                 Lakitu fishes us
                 up and back in Ghost Valley,
            respawn, reload,
            priority queueing
         TARS and Yoshi, Mario
      and Toad. Reach for
the skies and stars and
                    interlopers nope.

    And interlopers, nope.

Hitting the thinking ceiling
my content ululates.

And the county councillor
spits oats.

There are not plenty more fish in the sea.

Zero-sum

pedestrian muses

No Pence.

Continuous
deliverability.

A winning
formula.

A European
fucking passport.

You have zero boundaries.

    To bake an assertion
one must first emanate from the midst of Trudeau

Long-term healthy function
chewing on your futon

Let's all just stop
going to work, you know

See what goes down, see
what happens

Turn away, Frink
Literal giblets stay
in your lane

Haters alphabetically head us off
        now, enter
pleas, where the morning's
an emulsion
    with the sea:
               afterthought tailing
                    afterthought
over the bank with the storm.
The ire arc. An open mind.
Odour of hors d'oeuvres at weakest
    502 Bad Gateway
Lay in your stain.
Quorum sensing
    with a certain sprezzatura
            I rout accelerationism
None of my pets are breathing properly
@dril
        to nibble The Independent Group
    Evidence-based sophistry.
Bolsonaro and the things that made him
break up on re-entry
        on re-entry
I search for something or check
    out what's happening
    parallel to Blackpool Tower
taxpayers sashay past a distant gulf.
Ulterior as you decided to rewild your pet
continent, fucker,
        the arborescent hypertext behind
Urban Dictionary
            What year is this?
Out of the board meeting
into the board meeting.

Sheet lightning wrecked your dream
under the mulberry.
       Insert the microchip.
Sheet lightning

Ergo, I'll soon
                      connive to say adieu
    Prosodic skyscraper fabulously
To warm the globe
Where does any of this get us though?
              What's past is epilogue
    and last is climate justice
The presbyters are coming
for my lunch money, buddy
      Like I care
         Caning it
    An easy punchline
Cracking up in the
        wake of dawn
      We fell in love on Skype
                  a trillion years ago
        Neutrons on the pulse
and pretty workmanlike
      The spoon ran away with the dish
        This is my jam
Track changes
    winding in the blow

       They do quantity
  control
in the largesse
        labyrinth
   Moment form
   I've pleasured it from side to side
   Moment form
   I won the internet
when a lyre
starts to burn
   you give the lie to me
   Skimp on.

  Outbreaks of
    non-sequiturs
normalise on the edge of the event horizon
It got to me. It got to me.

We go long distance.
   All the people that drop out
       of a life
    Lost a stem cell in the cloud forest
      Choose your own addenda
   No spoilers.
   No truisms.
Winging it, Alexa
   Mutability is oil
Picking up the pieces, microdoses
     Meet cute fluted

        That's a British value
                Care I like
          All changes saved
    If you require a chinwag
           consult the weeping polls
Poetry has ruined me
                Let's make ends meet
                Let's make ends meet

Plucking up the storage
this is my preservative,
recognisably is
        now, now
Donald Trump baby balloon
    Mindfuck.
           Action that.
        I can't even.

What seems to be the
    problem here?
        You're tuned. Stay tuned.
            Keep up.
    Haze over a lifeway then

You're newsy, bloodletting the muses
            Get Out of Jail Free, taking
                the temperature, air
    miles and air miles. Get stuff
It bears repeating though, stay loose
        With odds
and ends, with such and such

With no clear loser
      on this hellsite
Turning back towards the leisure centre.

Now, now, lover
    in the climate riot. Fly
Emirates. Your email finds me well.
        Nuancing at once.
           Tucking into your placenta.
               These are voice notes
        but they're nothing
    and it's finally imposter syndrome time,
extinction in the face of this emotion
        I guess the feed dictates
    Wilding my drive
            Subprime, the microplastic
        monument to judge's bloodstream
          Please retain for your records
    timesaving trash life
That'll fettle it, publics
        Harshing my module
    urlz
    s.com/F
        LNU4
      Not to pack it in
Let steeples
enjoy things.

Slimline. Gulp
Lately skimming
        typos within typos

           Pyrrhic winners
stammering over the scanner
and I can't stress this enough
              a bliss immiscible
will make nothing endurable
Head-on, another smother
                   Colloid
        Into the big top
Triumphal stakeholders in our own retirement
      the last Avenger's
happy
wrack
        shreds Frontex
    I lost the internet

And then at last it fills your eyes, in prospect
the running jump out of the cash nexus
Conflagration. Listing of the
world-system
        tugged back, but

> Skyline
> warded off twice over, feeding
> forward. Wildfire under the
> pearling cumulus, on track,
> and they accumulate
> ICE.

> No borders. With self-help spurned
> the gastronaut hooks us up, lying to the end
> I haven't finished. Sickle cell
> liquidity and a prenup in Brentwood.
> Pyroclastic life hack.
> Recover. It wasn't that I necessarily felt
> more vilified than anyone else
> but the pricks from G4S manhandled my knapsack
> on the escalator. No matter. Queueing
> for a wristband at the Pleasure Beach in cod-atomic
> sleet, indifference propels you and reform of
> indifference propels you, normal
> news for the effectual. Kiss a pigeon on the
> wing, kiss a lesser black-backed gull
> Chewing more than you can bite off.
> So to speak. Snug as a bug in a rug. Satan we stan
> but so-and-so is such a desktop icon.
> Wow. An inlet. More power to you
> It fills me with regret to say
> that I must soon conclude my day

                        and eat the hand that feeds me

For the unforeseeable.

            On second thoughts
            spokespeople,
        better to rein in hell
make a chimera
              grate again
          save money, feel epic
          mania adjacent
having a complete beluga of a time
cool story bro
alighting on a subtweet, counterpunching liar
Elizabeth Holmes cajoles me, central defender
           Hail infernal words
           Paging another world
                 Typos within typos
                        Affirm
and lie, affirm
and lie. Normal news for the
        not more
                lamination language, time
                to specialise.

            Sippy cup ringfenced fantasia
            Sippy cup autorelic.

So to speak.

In the next segment what's the probability
a confirmed yuppie will fill out this packet of
    huge forms with neutral ease.
Kneejerk feathers compose themselves.
    Nobody's fantasy dissolves the Groupon.
My narcolepsy I acquired *in vitro*.
My signature remains a minute squiggle.

After rethinking the SUV, cousin
can return to timestamped panic
    The cherubim of Uber.

It's been tricky to remain untheorized
    so of course I failed.

There were those omissions.

Mr. Mime recoils,
rewires this rhyme

Share your
    location to locate your share
typed the influencer, before theologically scratching
    their name into the exit sign.
    An outlet.
Get over here and
    hold me.
You should see the PowerPoint.
You should set sail for the Hyades.
Lecturing the plastisphere
    boosterism's loose
        I wouldn't
        have nothing
if I didn't have you.
And the networker frets beneath meticulous
weather.
I'm getting there.
Challenges and opportunities at the
science-policy-society interface
Below a billow.
Confined in hateful offices, grey goo
pollutes our penultimate bottle of Grey Goose
Kyotan breezeblocks. Ask
what might it mean never to micromanage
        but do it
in your best impression of your nearest colleague

Kick a budgie in the face
Reappear without a trace

Is this thing on, pro skier

                  explaining my process
Paul Ryan declares a fucking thumb
        war with the centaurs
    My appendix spontaneously entrusted
to the dayglo pay cap
              I'm sucking up and listing things again.

    What the iCloud
           ducking in my rideshare
Keep the lyre burning
                Changeling climates
                as if
    language
        pointed
to its contentment.

I need to report
unauthorised access, earthing
              touch the sky.
The song is still in your pocket.
            Ark of endurance
mashed to the last
    We'll see.

                      And fine by me.
From time to time.
            And fine
    by me.

I have to go and do my roadworks.
    At record highs.

>   Now and again
> how to shift.
> >   A baby in my hopeful nope.
> >   I feel you.
> How to shift.
> >   And mine
> >   by fee.
> At record highs.

> Sippy cup
> planetary
> pronoun.

> How latterly electable of you.
> >   Too much or not too much

Sweep blissfully along me.
    A sky's a style.
It got to me. Lean into it.
        It got me like there's no tomorrow.
What's the forecast, windsurfing
           hyper-attentive
    from meantime to meantime
Shuffling through the planetariat
under the sponsorship of Hermes, coral bleaching
        what a relief
when it dusked
                      on me
with wishful thinking NGL
    on the play button
WALL-E scrubs and scrapes
into the clean-up beam me up
        loitering by the Shard
           in the miniscule
    comedy of a meme.
Blue screen.
Will hell tear this time.
        Wage freeze.
      Never reproduce these.
    All the blue ticks somersault over the
        candlestick, from zero
    to zero, from and to
  and a plane ticket
No pixels were spared in the tracing of this commons
        Reheat as we go
not yet bursting through the airport terminal
                through factory settings

to the aura of the third runway
                Front crawl
subdivisions of cooperative self-disgust.
                      Push through, people.
        Change the subject.

From the inset
                      credit where credit is due
              holographic polyp phoning
          home from the Millennium Dome
      the serotonin phone-in.
        An antifluxon.
        I default.
Beta blockers on the lucky Pendolino
in the chequered weather
        print screen tiny tab
            a spate of lovelyism
the utter joyful matter
scooping pylons in your nitrile gloves
the pylon pile-on.
        Your little hands.
About buffering
they were forever
        started so I'll finish
non-events shimmering half-life
calculate the damage, Worzel Gummidge.

> Crashes. A newsclip.
> Another newsclip.

> By now the time is telling me,
>   Eli Lilly.
> It's around here that it gets too
>   much to bear.
> No one listens but they
>   hear.

> The night is chill
>   and glows
>
>   now there's a nanosecond, Ludd, and it isn't
> shaken off. Sparklers. There's tear gas
>   at a distance, gaming
>   the system. I will never
> be fulfilled by any kind of work

At this conduit in the aleatory narrative
feeling jammed but
                            seeding
the song rings alphabetically
            for shits and giggles.
                    No kidding.
Stochastic magic purées word forms.
        Is this thing on
            or institutionally approved
                Go, go VW.

Well what did you really expect from your
third choice solar panel?
No forfeiting.
            Track the vectors
        Hermes lacerated
crudely
worse
thoughts along the Burma Plate
                torrenting at hyperspeed, seedling
        picketing Storm Emma
            Four real
                            jiggles
            and vaguely
off I fuck. Are you not overdone?
        I wish none of this had happened.

We can do it, *we're going together*
        85,000 new jobs. Foxconn
                        Spinning pinwheel.

>
> Tl;dr
>
> > you're off the hook
> > you're off the hook
>
> handing me my vital halo
> handing me my polar sandal
> > Where's the helipad
> > for real.

> I want to build a space to make you safe
>
>
> however momentary or fake.

So
>> prise the hour open
>>>> psychosomatically
and birthers and flat-earthers
>> tumble out of the charger port.
>> There's Murdoch. Nothing
>> accepts poets more
frictionlessly than this system.
>>>> Unsend.
>>>> Unfriend.
>> After all
>> I've got some real estate
here in my real estate
>> a couple of
dozen orca in Prince William Sound.
>>>> It's cool with me, Nick
>> in no danger
>> of thinking any more
A witness at
>> the opening of the file, Gazprom

>> Time is our tedious
>>>> ending
>> should here
>> have song
things. Keep on
things.

It follows the last phase of eventing
>> tickling Netflix
>> ex-seasonal the streams.
I call on the Clangers.

   Jobless but with a weakness
for social work in this
         to gather
      I show
myself a missing door or strike out
with the lofty software
   friendo,
       the final fracker self-immolates
     gets the latest over LazyTown

What salve
resolves never

    pacing onboard
      Serenity, nobody at last but
   me and the Athenians
and a plastic sachet of gnomes
        Chevron, Exxon
   sorry this is long.

These are drafts but they're something.
      Meltwater
optimises your story
     totalling
a morsel of
     the listicle
don't know.

                    Work out
Papa John's career in dog years
                            askance
big rigour
                    polonium toastie

            goes without saying
                            individual life
            passes from one end of agreement
            to the Arctic Circle when it is shaken.
                    Massed days
unformulated
                            sorry
this is wrong.

Give me your hand.

From the outset.

Trade slipstreams and shuck off the antiflux.

I never left.

More life.

A stanza floats into the foot spa, see
Irradiated tuck me in.
                  Thy wired client
           climbs inside a brioche bun
           though
Zippy departs solo. Scrolling
literally the degrees
                     lock it.

                Every other day, for now, I say
                           without going.

     It says without going.
Extractions
          after all.
Sorry this is long.

ACKNOWLEDGEMENTS

All books are alibis, but excerpts from this one have been published elsewhere. 'Entry Level' and 'Dust Mite' first appeared in issue 6 of *SPLINTER* magazine, 'Hit Counter' in issue 5 of *amberflora*, draft sections of 'Immaculate Blip' in the winter 2018 issue of *Botch* magazine, and the opening pages of 'The Noughties' in *summat* 1. Thanks are due to David Grundy, Gizem Okulu, Katy Lewis Hood, Pratyusha, Max Maher, and especially Tom Crompton and Alex Marsh for inviting Luke Roberts and I to read at the first of their *OUT ELSE* nights at SET in Dalston last year. Thanks also to Callie Gardner, Joe Luna, Sarah Bernstein and Dan Eltringham for organising readings in Edinburgh, Brighton, and Sheffield at which I was able to test drafts of 'The Noughties', and to Jessie Widner for designing the cover. *Scammer* was written to and for and with the encouragement of far too many friends, comrades, and real ones to name here, buoying me up through a difficult moment in my life, a rush of poniards and counters to spite the contemptible weather. You know who you are, and I love you all. Finally, this book wouldn't exist without Azad Ashim Sharma and Kashif Sharma-Patel of the87press, who do and have done so much for so many people. Thank you. See you in the next sphere.